CREATIVE
RITUAL

CREATIVE RITUAL

Combining YORUBA, SANTERIA, and WESTERN MAGIC TRADITIONS

El Obatala

SAMUEL WEISER, INC.

York Beach, Maine

Published in 1996 by
Samuel Weiser, Inc.
P. O. Box 612
York Beach, ME 03910-0612

02 01 00 99 98 97 96
10 9 8 7 6 5 4 3 2 1

Library of Congress Cataloging-in-Publication Data:
Helke, Thomas.
    Creative ritual / el Obatala.
        p.   cm.
    Includes bibliographical references (p.).
    1. Ritual. 2. Magic. 3. Occultism. I. Title.
BF1623.R6H43   1996
133.4'3--dc20   96-16319
                                                                        CIP

ISBN 0-87728-898-4
MG

Printed in the United States of America

Contents

Acknowledgments

May all those who inspired this book with their knowledge, love, and wisdom be thrice blessed with greater joy, fulfillment, and freedom in their lives:

Janice Nelson

Robert Hawkins

William Marlow

Eric Teissedre

Special thanks to my spirit guides
and to the Divine Consciousness

Preface

Every society has engaged in religious ritual. In this way, the ritual worker—shaman or priest—has kept alive the Inner Reality of life, itself, in the hearts of the people. This Inner Reality is the source of life. It doesn't matter what you term it—Christ, Krishna, Cosmic Power, Divine Principle, Atomic Equation—it is all the same thing. At this present stage of civilization, science is uncovering principles that shamans and priests have kept alive symbolically in ritual for aeons. The outer, objective world of science is beginning to recognize the inner, subjective world of mysticism.

Ritual is an integrative process that attunes the psyche to natural forces. In ritual, the inner mysteries, the divine principles, can be explored and made manifest in the life of the individual. Or ritual can be used in a very practical manner—through helping to fulfill specific desires. This book explains how to apply essential principles of ritual that were once held secret by shamans and priests.

The roots of the ritual magic described hereinafter have been harvested from several authentic sources. The primary sources are the religion of the Yoruba people of Nigeria and the cabalistic mystery tradition: I am an initiate of both traditions and can speak to you with confidence regarding certain forms of ritual magic. Although the two afore-mentioned religious traditions are derived from two diverse civilizations, there are strong undercurrents of like philosophy in both magical belief systems. In fact, the two systems complement each other rather nicely. Eclecticism is generally favored in the format of contemporary magical practitioners—it is helpful to broaden one's base from which to more effectively generate results.

In your hands, you now have the knowledge to become your own shaman or magician-priest, if you wish. Or you may use this information to explore subtle energy fields. Whatever your philosophical or religious inclination, the principles contained herein can help you to enhance any area of life. Apply this knowledge with love and wisdom and it will return the same to you.

Blessings of Light, Love, and Peace

Introduction

The information in this volume is yours to use as you will. The concepts, symbolism, and definitions are simplistic, and, with a little imagination and common sense, are easily adaptable to other philosophical and spiritual doctrines. Those doctrines with which you may be familiar, such as Jungian Psychology, Christianity, the Western Mystery Tradition, Hinduism, Buddhism, ancient religions, are all linked together by a common bond, a beneficent form of higher guidance. You may understand this higher guidance as "superconsciousness," "Christ," "the Higher Self," or "Divine Brilliance." Or you may have no particular spiritual or philosophical orientation. It makes no difference; with the principles set forth herein, you can commune with known subtle consciousness and energies. You may apply these principles to your own particular doctrine and thereby transform a distant dream into a more tangible reality, if you wish. Or, if you presently have no doctrine, you can create your own by recording the experiences gained in ritual. If you are as yet unfamiliar with ritual and spiritual experience, you will have a good working foundation on which to build.

Ritual or ritual magic is a profound form of auto-suggestion in which the psyche (subconscious mind) is rendered receptive to energy patterns. It is an ancient method of tapping known subtle energies that exist not only within each human being, but throughout the universe. Ritual magic can get you in touch with your inner self and the universal energies that permeate all life. For in ritual, both the inner and the outer are explored.

The principles of ritual in this book are applied to fulfilling specific individual desires. These principles may be applied in a broader sense, as in group rituals or by performing a ritual to help another. In the case of group ritual, one should lead the ritual while the others follow. With a little creative imagination, ritual can be applied to any problem.

Some of the terminology may be difficult to relate to your own way of thinking. This should not deter you from successfully performing a ritual for the terms are arbitrary, and are merely used as tools to explain a concept. One term that may present difficulty is "spiritual energy." This term refers to known subtle energies or divine beings, or both. In effect, it doesn't matter how you refer to the universal energies—as separate conscious beings (god, angels, spirits), archetypal subconscious forces, or physical energies—they will respond in the same way.

Read everything carefully. All the information you need to create and perform your own rituals is contained herein. Whatever your station in life, whatever your background in religion, philosophy, or metaphysics, you can apply the principles in this book and get results. If the general outline for performing ritual seems too difficult, use the Simple Ritual Format until you feel comfortable enough to apply more complex methods. Expensive supplies are not necessary; you can begin with one candle.

Don't overwork yourself with ritual; it is very potent, and too much ritual work can put a strain on the psyche. Perform ritual occasionally; use it to solve a special problem, or to gain an extra boost of energy. If you feel any sense of strain (mentally or physically) in any way, *then stop what you are doing* and refrain from doing any ritual work for awhile. It is fine to cast the circle of light and do something that will center you on yourself, as a simple prayer affirming the highest in your life, or a meditation in which your consciousness stays in your body. However, ritual work to produce a future effect (such as prayer, invocation, or meditation to get something) should be reserved for times of true need. Ritual is not meant to replace life, but it can be a way in which you can gain a greater understanding of the forces around you, as well as the forces within you.

Work within the light to help and to uplift others in some way (including yourself). Never try to control or bend the will of another with ritual, it will only bind you. If you decide to perform rituals for others, keep yourself protected in the white light so that you can remain psychically detached from your circumstances. Use your own judgement in charging a fee for your services; be reasonable if you do. It is believed that psychic or magical ability is eventually lost to materialism if money is charged for that ability. The other side of the coin preaches that, in the administration of spiritual services, an energy exchange of some kind must take place between client and counselor. If you follow the magical maxim, "As you give, so shall you receive," and give freely of yourself, the same (and perhaps more) will be returned to you some day. In this case, it does not seem unreasonable to request that the client purchase the supplies necessary for the ritual.

The principles in this book are based on tried and true methods. Feel free to experiment, but do so with good judgement; ritual is potent. The cosmic law—as you give, so shall you receive—applies very well here.

Verbatim rituals have purposely been omitted to avoid the stagnation of dogmatism and to allow you to be yourself. It is better that you create your own rituals based on your own experiences while utilizing the principles outlined in this book. In this way, you will grow quickly in experience and ability. You may use these principles exclusively, if you wish; they are based on experiences of true mystics, seers, and psychics. But let this book stand as a temporary guide, another step or signpost along the way. Eventually you will become your own teacher, guiding your own hand, initiating yourself into the greater mysteries of life through the medium of consciousness itself.

1

Ritual Basics

Ritual practice is enjoyable and easy once you thoroughly know and understand all the rudiments involved. And, when a ritual is properly executed, you will come away from it feeling refreshed and enlivened. The only way for you to know precisely how to enact a complete and effective ritual is by reading the entire book before you begin. If you are a beginner, you may feel there is a lot of metaphysical theory to grasp, but, once you have learned exactly how to perform a ritual from beginning to end, the implementation is easy. When you are finally ready to create your own rituals, you will find that all the techniques described herein are important for you to know and use. Chapter 4, Complete Ritual Outline, includes all the essential ritual techniques described in this volume and provides you with easy step-by-step instructions which you can follow each time you wish to create and perform a ritual.

Psychic cleanliness and balance are important preliminaries to all ritual work. In this way, you will bring clarity and strength to your rituals. Psychic cleanliness and balance are achieved by taking a salt water bath or *smudging* (if a bath is not possible) and then casting the circle of light in your ritual working area. You will begin by learning how to cleanse your physical body, your psychic energy field (which is your aura), and the ritual working area of negative, disharmonious energy.

Psychic Cleanliness

It is a common procedure to take a salt water bath before you begin a ritual. Thus, the negative or unwanted energy is banished and the ritual worker is free to bring more desirable energies forth. Simply add a generous dash of salt to your bath water. This will physically and psychically cleanse the body. If, for any reason, you cannot take the requisite pre-ritual bath, you may substitute a technique used by Native American Indians, called *smudging* or *smoking*. To smudge, place a small handful of whole sage (Salvia officinalis) on an oven-proof dish or seashell. Light the clump of sage until it begins to smolder. Then hold the dish or shell in front of you, being careful not to burn yourself in the process. (The dish or shell may become very hot.) Now waft the smoke gently towards you: first, pass some over your head and down your back, then pass some of the smoke to both arms, then to both legs; finally, brush the smoke four times to your heart area. Now you are smudged. Smudging generally provides as much psychic cleanliness as a salt water bath; however, I prefer the bath because it helps to put me in a more relaxed, receptive state of mind. You must do what you feel is best for you at the time, and it is perfectly permissible to do both. (In this case, take the salt water bath first, then smudge.)

The space in which you perform a ritual should be private, quiet, and clean. In order to cleanse, balance, and quiet the space psychically, a circle is cast. The symbol of the circle abounds in cultures throughout the world: it is the medicine wheel of the North American Indians, the mandala and prayer wheel of the Tibetans, the round table of the Arthurian Mysteries, the zodiac, the zero. To all these cultures it symbolizes the first manifestation, the beginning and the end. The circle is a bridge between two worlds, the spiritual and material; its presence creates a synthesis of oneness, wholeness, balance, and completion. For the ritual worker, it symbolizes the universe. Once the circle is cast, the ritual worker's consciousness becomes the center of that universe.

The Circle of Light

The circle is a powerful energy image; whatever is represented within that image with concerted effort becomes a real force that must find expression in the outer world once the circle is dissolved. Being both psychically protective and spiritually uplifting, the circle is a necessary element and the foundation of most ritual work.

When the Circle of Light is cast, a transmitter of power and communication is created between yourself and the subtle universal forces. You become the center of a symbolic sphere, as an individual planet with consciousness. The natural forces of the universe automatically respond to this symbol with energies of wholeness, balance, oneness, completion, and unity. The primary channel of these energies is consciousness. Your thoughts, feelings, invocations, and symbols are extensions of consciousness through which the universal energies become manifest. It is important to take into careful consideration what you represent in the circle and how you represent it. At least some degree of receptivity is necessary—to doubt what you are doing blocks the natural flow of subtle energies.

The circle may simply be visualized, created by an act of will. The boundaries of the circle may also be marked with chalk, salt, rope, or candles.[1] The size of the circle rests on individual preference; however, nine feet is a standard diameter. It may be larger or considerably smaller, but must be large enough in which to do some ritual work, even if the circle is used only to light a candle.

To cast the circle, first decide upon its size, then stand before (or look toward) its eastern arc. Pause momentarily in silent reverence of the Highest in your spiritual philosophy (as God, Light, Love, Starry Heaven, Cosmic Power, Divine Principle, Absolute Wisdom, Olofi, Christ, Mohammed, Great Spirit, Allah, Krishna, Zeus, El, Jah, Aum), whatever

---

[1]Figure 1 on page 4, figure 2 on page 5, and figure 9 on page 38 will show you different ways to cast the circle.

Start here

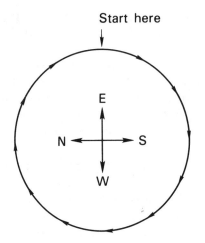

Figure 1. Creating a circle.

you deem to be the Highest. Then declare you are creating the circle with white fire[2] in the name of the Highest, such as:

> In the name of the Almighty
> I create this circle
> with white fire.

Next indicate the boundaries of the circle by tracing its perimeter in the air around you—use your index finger, an incense stick, or a wand as shown in Figure 1. Move in a clockwise direction, starting in the east and ending in the east. As you draw the circle, visualize brilliant, luminous, white flames blazing up wherever you trace its boundaries. If the circle is too small to include yourself, simply invoke or visualize white fire around yourself as well as the circle. Then sit, stand, or kneel, facing east, before your altar if you have

---

[2]White fire has no physical properties; in fact, it is cool and refreshing when experienced. If it seems too difficult to visualize white fire, white light may be visualized in its place. White light is also brilliant, luminous, cool, and refreshing; white fire (or astral fire) is simply the active form of white light. Both have an uplifting, refreshing effect on the psyche.

one (see figure 2). Now dedicate the circle to Light, or to Light and Love, or any suitable name of God, as:

> I dedicate this circle
> to Love and the white fire.
> So be it.

Use whatever feels right or is most meaningful to you. Now that the circle is cast, you are ready to begin the ritual.

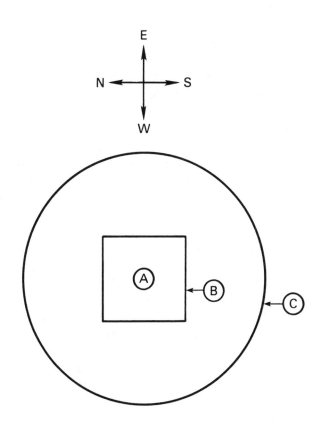

Figure 2. The circle in its simplest form. Here you see a) the desire candle (that represents the spiritual energy you wish to contact), b) the altar and/or your altar cloth, and c) the perimeter of your circle. The boundaries can be imaginary or you can physically mark them.

Ritual Format

Anyone can perform a ritual effectively. The prime ingredient is sincere intention. Without belief, receptivity to spiritual energy is blocked. Whether you call it receptivity or auto-suggestion matters not; without some belief, there will be no results. So open your mind a bit (and your heart) and let yourself experience something beautiful.

Ritual may be performed without any physical object, by visualization. However, most people prefer to use physical objects which help to focus the mind on the task at hand. In this case, there is one object that is most important in ritual—a candle. Other physical accoutrements—incense, divination materials, elemental tools—give rituals greater depth.

Whether you are a beginnr or very advanced, you will find the following basic format effective in designing any ritual for any purpose. All you need is a candle. (See Candles and Incense on page 35.) The candle is placed near the center of the circle. Clearly vocalize what you will do in the ritual, even if you are alone. (You may whisper your intention for performing the ritual if there are other people within hearing range who are not involved in performing the ritual.) Then cast the circle and sit, stand, or kneel before your altar (if it only be comprised of the candle), facing east. Contemplate the spiritual energy you wish to contact—as angel, pagan god, abstract principle, spiritual guidance, meditation/healing energies. (See Table of Correspondences on page 49.) Next light the candle with an appropriate invocation. Embellish the invocation, make it attractive, inviting, and sympathetic to the spiritual energy you invoke. Contemplate that spiritual energy: see it and feel it enter the circle as a living reality. You can imagine the spiritual energy any way you like—as a colored light; an anthropomorphized god form; a feeling of warmth or love; or a symbol that appropriately represents the spiritual energy you wish to contact. When you instinctively know that you have visualized or empathized the spiritual energy to a sufficient degree, address the energy with an appropriate verbal affirmation, question, or prayer. From this point you may continue or end the ritual as you see fit. The remainder of the ritual may require an offering, prayer, or meditation, in accordance with the spiritual energy contacted.

The concept is to create vibrations with mental/emotional projections, invocations, and symbols that will attract sympathetic spiritual energies. This is sometimes referred to as "sympathetic magic." It is a known cosmic law—like attracts like.

For example, perhaps you wish to enhance your routine meditation or daily prayer with a subtle energy. Invoking white fire would be appropriate because white fire is balanced, psychically protective, and uplifting. For this ritual, a white candle is most desirable. Place the candle near the center of the circle. State out loud what you will do in the ritual, as:

> I will invoke the white fire
> to enhance my meditation [or prayer].

Now cast the circle and sit, stand, or kneel, facing east, before the candle. Dedicate the circle to the Highest in your philosophy, as prescribed. In silence, momentarily contemplate the white fire. Then light the candle with a suitable invocation, as:

> By the Higher Power that is in me.
> I call upon the white fire,
> the Eternal Light that is pure and radiant,
> to enter this circle and strengthen my meditation now.

See the white fire enter the circle and fill it with shimmering radiance. (You may visualize this with your eyes open or closed.) When you feel the white fire has been sufficiently visualized, affirm its presence in the circle, as:

> I affirm the presence of the white fire
> in this circle now.

You may now proceed with your routine meditation or daily prayer. When you have finished praying or meditating, release the white fire from the circle with gratitude, as:

Thanks be to the white fire
for entering this circle and
blessing my meditation [or prayer].
I now release the white fire
from the boundaries of this circle.
So be it.

Extinguish the candle here.

Now that the ritual is ended, you must dissolve the circle. This is a necessary procedure that allows expression of the invoked spiritual energy in the outer world. To dissolve the circle, once again move in a clockwise direction. Make a symbolic gesture of creating an opening in the circle, of breaking the link: open a door or window in the room or pass your hand around the perimeter of the circle as though opening a curtain.

Throughout the procedure, the ritual worker should maintain a worshipful or reverent attitude toward the spiritual energy which is to be contacted. In this way, the deeper levels of the psyche are awakened. There will be greater receptivity to subtle energies, and that which is to be contacted will respond to a sincere and respectful manner. You will instinctively know if you have performed the ritual effectively. The more you perform ritual, the greater your intuition becomes. If a particular room is continually used for ritual work, treat that room with special reverent respect. It will become imbued with psychic energy. After a time, others will be able to feel this energy, too.

You must practice and experience ritual before you can truly know and understand it.

Simple Ritual Format

Here is an easy ritual that you can perform until you feel comfortable using the more complex forms of ritual discussed in this book. This form is also good for emergency situations when time does not allow for a more involved ritual.

Visualize (or imagine) a circle (or a bubble of white or golden light) around yourself, up to nine feet in diameter. Light a white candle and say:

> Blessed is the light of spirit.
> May it protect me and uplift me
> now in this circle of light.

Then say the Lord's Prayer, or any suitable prayer that gives you a feeling of universal love or holiness. After the prayer, ask for whatever it is that you desire (such as protection, love, peace, financial help, health). Now contemplate that which you desire, visualize it entering the circle of light and becoming a present influence in your life. Do the visualization as long as it is comfortable for you. After the visualization, say:

> Thanks be to Spirit for entering this circle
> and blessing it with the light.

Extinguish the candle. Then say:

> I declare this circle now open
> and all forces now free.
> So mote it be.

The ritual is ended.

This form of ritual is effective; however, the more complex forms get the mind more involved in the ritual by inspiring the imagination, and thereby aid in channeling spiritual energy.

Ritual Timing

The best time to perform ritual is when you are in a good mood or when it feels like the right time. Then you are in greater harmony with the flow of the universe and you will naturally have a greater supportive power for your ritual.

To attract a specific energy or influence to you, use the waxing moon period (from new moon to full moon). To banish or psychically cleanse an atmosphere of negative or unwanted energy, use the waning moon period (from full moon to new moon). Some believe it is wise to banish negative influences before attracting new, more desirable energies. Avoid performing rituals on the last three days before the new moon. The local newspapers usually indicate the phases of the moon in the weather section, or you may purchase an astrological ephemeris or calendar.

There are specific times during the day when the natural energy tides are more conductive to ritual work than at other times. For more information on the energy tides, consult the Suggested Reading List on page 65. However, for now, it is perhaps best to apply the above rules. In an emergency situation, the above rules may be allayed for the time.

Perform a ritual for as many days as you like, until you obtain that which you desire from the ritual. Or follow a pattern and perform the same ritual for three, four, seven, or nine consecutive days or weeks (in this case, once each week). You can also use the symbolic numbers as they correspond to the specific spiritual energies shown in the Table of Correspondences. (Perform the ritual for that number of days.)

Allow time for your magic to work. It may manifest immediately, but it is likely to take a week or longer for you to see results. Magic is a natural art and science dealing with subtle, natural forces, both inner and outer. Therefore, the magic you perform in ritual will manifest in a very natural manner. Ritual magic will not do everything for you; you must do your part, too. If you ritualize for money, then you must use all your constructive resources outside of the ritual to obtain the money you want. Your magic will certainly make the effort easier for you. Don't be surprised with any dramatic results from your magic; with attentive practice, this can become an almost common occurrence. Put yourself in a position that will allow your magic to become manifest. For example, if you want a lover and perform a ritual to get a lover, don't shut yourself away at home, expecting the perfect lover to knock on your door. Everything is possible, but it would be better for you to get out and be with people in some way—that prince in shining armor or goddess of your dreams might be out there waiting to sweep you off your feet! In this case, if you lack confidence to be with people, it might be a good idea to perform a ritual for greater confidence or self-esteem before asking for a lover.

Once you have performed a ritual, let it be; don't try to predict the way in which your magic will become manifest. Let the higher creative intelligence decide that. Don't talk about the ritual you perform until some time after you have received definite results. To discuss your magic only serves to disperse the energies you have set in motion. Silence is golden. Simply do your part outside the ritual by making yourself available in logical situations that will better allow your magic to work.

Review of Ritual Format

1. Ascertain the kind of spiritual energy that will best answer your needs. Refer to the Table of Correspondences on page 49.

2. Affirm what you will do in the ritual, then cast the circle of light around yourself in a clockwise direction.

3. Sit, stand, or kneel, facing east before the candle which represents the spiritual energy you wish to contact.

4. Light the candle and make an invocation to the spiritual energy you are contacting.

5. Visualize the spiritual energy entering the circle and fulfilling your desire.

6. When you feel the spiritual energy is in the circle, vocally affirm its presence. Know that it will fulfill your desire.

7. Thank the spiritual energy for entering the circle and answering your request (even if it is not yet evident that your wish has been granted).

8. Extinguish the candle.

9. Dissolve the circle.

2

Divination

Divination is a technique that can be used for communicating with divine consciousness through the subconscious mind. It enhances the ritual process by tuning the psyche into what is happening spiritually. It relays objective information about the specific spiritual energy you have invoked after you have cast the circle. After an invocation has been made, it is most desirable to determine the kind of spiritual energy that has entered the circle (whether it is the energy that has been invoked, another energy, or none at all). Divination will determine this. The divination response you get will also determine your next step in the ritual (whether to continue with divination or proceed to the next logical step in the ritual).

Divinatory Method

Although other appropriate questions may come to mind during a ritual, there are four basic questions with which to be most concerned. They are:

Who is there? This question determines who or what has entered the circle after an invocation has been made. If you invoked the goddess Venus to bring you good luck, you might ask the question as, "Who is in the circle now, is it Venus?" or, "Who is in the circle now, is it the one whom I invoked?" If you get a negative response at this point, you are free to close the ritual, or you may continue—perhaps Divine Intelligence has deemed another spiritual energy more suitable for your intended purpose in creating the ritual. If you decide to continue after receiving a negative response, ask the basic question again. This time specify another spiritual energy or being that you feel could answer your wish in the ritual. For instance, "Who is in the circle now, is it Jupiter?" (The god Jupiter also bestows good luck.) Again you may get a negative response, but you are free to continue asking about other energies or beings that may have been attracted to the circle. Or you may discontinue the ritual at this point. Several negative responses should indicate to you that this is not a particularly good time to perform this ritual (see Ritual Timing on page 9). Or perhaps you omitted an important ingredient somewhere along the way. (Did you open the circle correctly? Was your invocation to the spiritual energy attractive and inviting? Do you believe in what you are doing?) When an affirmative answer has been obtained, ask the next divination question.

Why did you come? Now that the spiritual energy has been determined, it is desirable to know if it has come to grant your request. If you had invoked Venus to bring you her gift of luck and you have verified her presence in the circle (through divination), you might ask, "Why is Venus in this circle now, is it to bring me her gift of luck?" Again, if you get a negative response to the question, you may discontinue the ritual (this time with thanks to Venus for entering the circle). However, it might be wiser to ascertain why Venus entered the circle— perhaps she wants to bring you a greater gift. When you have determined why the spiritual energy/being has entered the circle, continue with the next question.

What is needed from me to make this happen? Suppose you ascertained that Venus brought her gift of luck to you; then she would probably want something from you in return. Usually an energy exchange of some kind is required by the gods and other spiritual energies before they will help you. This may be in the form of a poem, song, or dance— something that will come from deep within you and is sincerely felt. Sometimes a flower or piece of fruit is requested. Or it could be any combination of things. To determine what kind of offering is required, you might ask the question as, "What is needed from me to make this happen—a love poem?" If you get a negative response, keep asking what is wanted. A song, a dance, an orange or some other exchange that you will think of may be appropriate. When you receive an affirmative answer, give what is requested then and there, if at all possible. If it is a poem, write the poem and recite it. Don't be surprised if you feel creatively inspired, let it happen. If a physical object is requested (as an orange or flowers), place it gently on the altar or altar cloth, with a reverent gesture (a bow of the head, for instance). If it is not within your range of possibility to make the required offering, do not break the circle to make it happen. (For example, if an orange has been requested and there is one in the refrigerator—don't run and get it.) Instead, ask if you may give the offering at a more convenient time or ask if there is anything you can offer in its place now. (Normally some agreement can be reached.) Sometimes a spiritual energy/being will require nothing from you; some only desire to serve. However you conceptualize the spiritual energy or being you invoke—as an abstract principle or a living conscious being—show it due veneration. This form of treatment will produce the most rewarding results. Whether you consider the spiritual energy to be an aspect of your own subtle consciousness or a separate living being with its own consciousness, you are dealing with real forces that must be respected (just as gravity and electricity are respected). After a suitable offering has been made, ask the next question.

Was the offering acceptable? When an offering has been agreed upon and you have given the offering to the spiritual energy, you must know if the offering has been accepted. As your divination question, you might simply ask, "Was the offering acceptable?" If not, ask if you should offer more of what you had previously offered, or if you could improve upon what you had offered (perhaps with more sincere intent). Or ask if anything else is desired. If your offering has been accepted, you may assume your original request will be granted. When you receive an affirmative answer, end the ritual with thanks to the spiritual energy for entering the circle and granting your request. Thank all other spiritual energies/beings that may have been attracted to your circle. The closing statement of thanks might be worded as, "Thanks be to the beautiful Venus for blessing this circle of light with her gift of luck. And thanks be to all other spirits who revealed their light and blessings in this circle. Blessed is the light of spirit." Now dissolve the circle. (See Ritual Format, page 8.)

• • •

If you did not complete the ritual because the desired spiritual energy or being did not enter your circle, or did not come to fulfill your original request, you may try again, perhaps the next day. You may attempt to contact a specific energy or being until you get what you want. Sometimes the child who cries the longest gets the most attention! After a reasonable length of time or number of tries, if you have not received the kind of help you think you need, try a different approach to the problem. It could be that another spiritual energy is a better solution (see Table of Correspondences on page 49). Divination should help you make a beeline to the source of any problem. Ritual is not meant to eradicate all other sources of problem-solving and help in day-to-day living, but it is meant to enhance and direct existent powers and abilities in the life of the individual. If you find that your ritual work is still not helping in just the way you like or need, it is perfectly alright to consult a priest, medical doctor, psychological counselor, or friend. It does not mean that you are an inept person if you consult another for help; perhaps you have a little energy or psychological blockage somewhere that interferes with your ritual work. Ritual takes practice, like anything else, to become good at it. Very few people on this planet can solve all their own problems through ritual. No man or woman is an island, so it behooves us all to share our problems and lives with one another. Some people solve their own problems by helping others solve problems. If you have a friend who is interested in ritual work, you might ask your friend to do the ritual for you; sometimes amazing results are obtained using this method. The best thing is to experiment and see what works best for you. In the case of a medical problem (especially a serious one), consult a physician, then perform a ritual to amplify the healing process.

Once you feel comfortable with the divination process, don't limit yourself to the four basic divination questions. Allow yourself to be creative and imaginative. Any question can be answered through divination; however, ask questions appropriate to the spiritual energy invoked. When divinating, it is not uncommon to receive psychic messages—intuitive feelings in the stomach area or thoughts in the head. Pay attention to these messages; it is often the Divine communicating to you through the subconscious mind about the question asked in divination. Common sense will tell you if the message is valid or not.

Divination adds greater life and meaning to ritual through attunement of the psyche to the spiritual energy at hand.

Divinatory Objects

There are many tools that may be used for divination; however, the simpler forms are most effectively adapted for use in ritual, such as: divination with cowry shells, a pendulum, or a regular deck of playing cards. Natural materials, such as wood, stone, or bone, are preferred for divination. Consecrate the divination tools you decide to use (see Consecration of Ritual Objects on page 23).

More than one divination tool can be used when asking the questions. For instance, for the question, "Why did you come?" you might wish to use a tarot card layout. This would give you the answer "why" without going through all the yes and no possibilities with cowry shells or the pendulum. However, for a more obviously yes or no question, such as, "Was the offering acceptable?" the cowry shells or pendulum would be fine.

Once you have acquired expertise with divination, you might wish to utilize other divination tools. For now, so as not to confuse you, the discussion will be limited to the use of the three previously mentioned forms.

Divination with Cowry Shells

For the following simple form of divination, any four objects of like substance may be used which will yield a yes/no response when they are tossed or cast. Cowry shells are my favorite divinatory tools because they are attractive, easy to handle, and have a natural link with the powerful ocean. (See figure 3.) Cowry shells, or money cowry (*cypraea moneta*), are found in Australia, the Indian Ocean, and the Pacific Islands. Money cowry was once a ready-made currency that was popular among world merchants and aboriginal tribes. Presently, cowries are traditional divinatory tools of the Yoruba people of Nigeria as well as practitioners of the Santeria religion here in the Americas. Although the priesthood of the Yoruba often use a sixteen-shell toss in their divinations, a four-shell toss is quite adequate for ritual work. Money cowry, which range in color from white to canary yellow, and vary in length from two-thirds to one-and-one-half inches, can be obtained from some import stores (at a

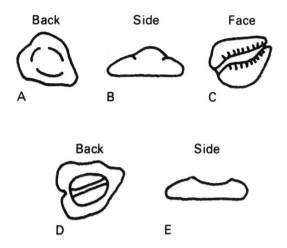

Figure 3. Cowry shells. A, B, and C show you the back, side and face of the shell. You need to remove the bubble-like protuberance from all the shells. Use a wire cutter or a nail clipper. By doing this, the shells will have two relatively flat surfaces on which to fall when you toss them. D and E show what the shell should look like when you have removed the bubble.

nominal price) or in its natural habitat. If you cannot acquire four cowries of approximately the same size, coins of equal denomination can be substituted for comparable accuracy.

When four shells or coins are used for divination, there are five possible combinations or responses. They are:

2 up/2 down: this is a definite "yes" response to the question and no further divination is necessary in reference to that question.

3 up/1 down: this is a "yes" response to the question; however, further divination is suggested in reference to that question—there is more to be learned.

4 up: this is a definite "yes" response to the question. It also holds a special blessing from the Divine to the querist in reference to the question.

3 down/1 up: this is a "no" response to the question; however, further divination is suggested in reference to the question.

4 down: this is a definite "no" response to the question; no further divination is suggested in reference to the question.

To divinate, hold the shells (stones, or coins) between your hands and verbalize your question. (It must be one that will elicit a yes or no response.) Pause momentarily, then shake the shells in your hands (like dice) and toss them before you. Check the list of combinations above to read the answer. Figure 4 illustrates a yes answer using the cowry shells.

You will notice in this form of divination there are three "yes" combinations and two "no" combinations. Also, cowry shells have an irregular shape; therefore, they are not proportionately weighted. In spite of these imbalances, I have found the divination process to be satisfactory. To remedy the problem of irregular shape and weight, coins or stones of equal size, weight, and shape may be substituted.

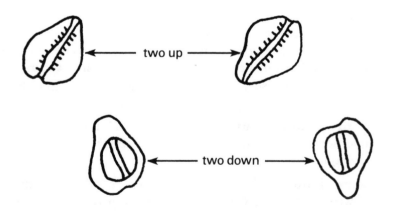

Figure 4. A divinatory toss. Here we see a "yes" answer: 2 up/2 down.

Divination by Playing Cards

If you find the 4-shell form of divination to be inconvenient, you may use an ordinary deck of playing cards to divinate. For the playing card divination, start with a new deck of playing cards. Bless the cards and use them only for divination. Predetermine one color to symbolize "yes" and the other color to symbolize "no." To avoid future psychic confusion, let this be a permanent decision. To divinate, ask the question, shuffle the cards (for as many times as you like) and cut them. Take the first three cards from the top of the deck and turn them over—these cards will yield your answer. Hearts and diamonds (red cards) are "yes" and clubs and spades (black cards) stand for "no." The following combinations are possible:

3 red: emphatic yes.

2 red/1 black: yes, keep asking.

1 red/2 black: no, keep asking.

3 black: emphatic no.

Pendulum Divination

For pendulum divination, attach a small weighted object (such as a ring or crystal) to a piece of thread several inches long. Hold the top of the thread between your thumb and index finger, while the weighted object hangs freely beneath your hand. Hold your hand still—the pendulum will swing by itself, motivated by subtle body movements. Let a back-and-forth swinging motion represent "yes" and a side-to-side swinging motion represent "no." After you ask the divination question, notice which way the pendulum swings to obtain the answer. With practice the pendulum can be a reliable divination tool. As with playing cards, bless the pendulum. In the blessing, state that a back-and-forth motion means "yes" and a side-to-

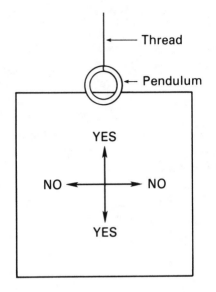

Figure 5. The Pendulum. Draw a diagram indicating the "yes" and "no" swinging motions. Place the diagram on a level surface and hold the pendulum over the center of the diagram when you divinate.

---

side motion means "no." You may draw a diagram that will better clarify the two motions for the subconscious mind. Place the diagram on a level surface and hold the pendulum over the center of the diagram while you divinate (see figure 5).

Consecration of Ritual Objects

To consecrate something is to make it holy, by psychically charging it with energy and a benediction. Blessing ritual objects better prepares them for use in ritual by aligning their vibrations with spiritual energies.

To consecrate any object, place it on your left hand and put your right hand over the object. Hold the object thusly in front of your solar plexus (which is your power center). Concentrate on energy circulating around your body and through the object a few times. Then visualize brilliantly luminous white fire entering the object and filling it with the fire and light. Now you must do a psychic cleansing and then bless the object, such as:

> I hereby cleanse this [object] with the white fire.
> Now I bless it in the name of the Highest [God, Christ, Krishna, Allah, Olofi, Great Spirit, Love].
> So be it.

Use whatever benediction appeals to you. Make the blessing uplifting so that the vibrations of the object are lifted up into the light and the higher spiritual vibrations. First banish the object of unwanted or negative energy, then bless it with the good or higher energy.

You might wish to consecrate an object for a specific purpose as it is used in your ritual work. In this case, state that you are blessing the object for a particular purpose in the blessing affirmation. For instance, perhaps you decide to have a statue of Saint Michael on your altar to aid you in healing work. In this case, you would hold the statue between your hands and visualize the white fire and bless the statue, as:

> In the name of God [or Christ], I hereby banish all negative and unwanted energy from this statue of Saint Michael with the white fire. Now, in the name of God [or Christ], I bless this statue with the magnificent healing power of Saint Michael. So mote it be.

You can make the blessing longer or shorter, suited to your own concepts and beliefs, as you see fit.

Objects that are used repeatedly in your rituals (such as altarpieces, symbols, elemental weapons, incense, and candle holders) should be consecrated. After the first consecration of an object, no further consecrations are necessary. Keep blessed objects in a safe place so that they are not handled by others who have nothing to do with your ritual work. Blessed objects should only be used for ritual work, never for common use.

To make holy water, add a dash of salt to a glass of water and bless it as described on page 23.

Divination Ritual Format

The following is a ritual using divination. Four cowry shells are used to divinate. The intention of the ritual is softly vocalized: "I am here to contact my spirit guides for healing, new direction, and change in my life." The circle of light is cast and the ritual worker kneels before the altar, contemplating momentarily the spiritual energy he or she wishes to contact. Then the candle on the altar is lit (see figure 2 on page 5) with this invocation: "I call my spirit guides to me now to help me with healing, new direction, and change in my life." The ritual worker visualizes spiritual guidance entering the circle to help with the request. When it is felt that spiritual guidance has been sufficiently visualized, the following divination procedure may ensue ("Q" is the example question asked by the ritual worker; "A" is the answer one ritual worker received by divination):

Q: Who is in the circle now; is it my spirit guides?

A: Three down/one up (see Divination with Cowry Shells, page 19, to read the answers).

Q: Is it Venus? (The ritual worker felt it might be Venus from experience in past rituals.)

A: Two up/two down.

Q: Why is Venus here? Is it to help me with my personal power? (The ritual worker knew, through past divination, that Venus is a personal power source.)

A: Three up/one down.

Q: (At this point the ritual worker decided to continue the ritual with Venus, in place of his spirit guides, because Venus was able to help him in the past.) What would Venus have me do for my personal power, a power song?

A: Two up/two down. (Here the ritual worker sang a "power song" to Venus. It consisted of sounds evoked from his creative imagination that were chanted rhythmically.)

Q: Was the singing good for Venus? (*i.e.*, "Was the offering acceptable?")

A: Two up/two down.

From this point, the ritual worker could have continued the ritual or ended it with thanks to Venus and then dissolved the circle. Further divination could have been pursued in the light of Venus' presence; however, it was not necessary. Subjectively speaking, the ritual worker left this ritual feeling enlivened, refreshed, more self-confident, and with a sense of renewed inner strength. Although he did not contact the spiritual beings he thought he needed (*i.e.*, the spirit guides), his request was granted through another spiritual energy source.

• • •

When you perform a ritual, be confident to invoke whatever energy appeals to you (Christ, angels, gods, spirit guides, healing energies). The more you align your consciousness with that which you invoke, the better are your chances of attracting that energy to your circle. You may find that one particular energy comes to you more than any other, or there may be a particular energy that you enjoy working with and that is easier for you to contact. If so, pay attention, take the time to understand why—through divination or your own intuition—it could be important energy for you. Every person has an individual attunement to the cosmic energies. Some people are more attuned to the love energy, some are more attuned to healing, while others are more attuned to the energies of white light and peace. (The basic spiritual or cosmic energies are listed in the Table of Correspondences on page 55. You might discover which energies best describe your highest ideals by using this list.)

Review of Divination

1. Divination is used to communicate with the Divine about the spiritual energy in the circle.

2. Divination is begun after the spiritual energy has been invoked and visualized.

3. In ritual, there are four main questions with which to be concerned:

Who is there?—ascertains the specific kind of energy that has entered the circle after an invocation has been made.

Why did you come?—ascertains whether the energy entered the circle to fulfill your wish.

What is needed from me to make this happen?—to fulfill a wish, a spiritual energy often requires an offering from the ritual worker (as a dance, song, or a flower).

Was the offering acceptable?—ascertains whether the spiritual energy has accepted what has been offered. If there is a yes response to the question, the wish will be fulfilled in some way. If there is a no response, ask what can be done to improve upon the offering.

4. There are many forms of divination; any may be used. A simple and effective form is the "four-shell" divination. Any four objects may be used that will render a yes or no response when tossed. With four such objects there are five possible responses:

2 up/2 down = yes.

3 up/1 down = yes, but keep asking.

4 up = emphatic yes.

3 down/1 up = no, but keep asking.

4 down = emphatic no.

5. With the four-shell divination any other questions may be asked throughout the ritual as it pertains to the spiritual energy at hand.

6. When the ritual worker feels satisfied that, through divination, the original request has been or will be fulfilled in some way, the ritual may be ended and the circle dissolved.

7. Special thanks are always given to any and all spiritual energies that may have entered the circle of light during the ritual.

3

Materia Magica

The subconscious mind is the psychic bridge between you and the subtle universal forces you will contact when you perform a ritual. It is necessary to gain the cooperation of the subconscious mind in your ritual work because it is the subconscious mind that contacts and helps to manifest the spiritual energies in the physical world. Your subconscious mind will become interested and responsive in the ritual you will perform when it perceives that your conscious intention is sincere. To impress your subconscious mind to work for you, make every thought, sight, sound, and movement connected with your ritual definitely and deliberately focused on the spiritual energy you would like to manifest. In this way, the conscious mind is concentrated on a single purpose and the subconscious mind, which is directed by the conscious mind, will respond in like manner.

The subconscious mind is aware of the directives of the conscious mind through thought and the five senses. When you charm the subconscious mind through these avenues of awareness, it literally becomes fascinated into attending to the task you have set for it. The more effectively you involve your physical senses with your rituals, the more you will capacitate your subconscious mind (and the higher spiritual forces) to help produce the results you want. There are three primary senses with which to be most concerned. They are: the visual (sight), auditory (hearing), and kinesthetic (sense of touch or feelings of muscle movement). The olfactory (smell) and gustatory (taste) senses are of secondary importance, although the olfactory sense is satisfied when you burn incense.

Essentially, by following the instructions outlined in this book, you will be enchanting your mind through a large portion of your sensory awareness when you perform a ritual: the beautiful altar arrangement and soft, flickering candlelight will captivate the subconscious mind through the sense of sight; the sound of your own voice as you deliver a paced invocation will entrance the mind through the sense of hearing; and, the slow, measured bodily movements you enlist as you light the candles and incense will enthrall the subconscious mind through the kinesthetic sense. Similarly, when you have obtained the cooperation of your vastly intelligent, talented, and powerful subconscious mind, it will be easier for you to get the results you want from your rituals. This concept is wise to consider when selecting ritual supplies and setting up your altar.

Ritual supplies need not be elaborate or expensive to be effective. Good results can be obtained with very few supplies. Whatever you decide to use should have a practical purpose that pertains specifically to the ritual you will perform. For example: in a ritual to stimulate creativity in the arts, you would want to use only that which symbolizes or pertains specifically to the Sun (the Sun generally rules the Arts—see Table of Correspondences, page 59). A scarab, yellow candle, frankincense, "The Sun" (XIX) tarot card, an orange-colored cloth, and some oranges (for an offering) are appropriate symbols of the Sun.

You may equip your magical theater any way you like, just be certain to set the stage fittingly for the specific spiritual energy and divine being you will summon. Let your altar and ritual working area be a semblance of simplicity, order, and beauty.

The Altar

The altar is the center of activity within the circle and, therefore, should be placed in the center. Otherwise, the altar may be kept against a wall, out of the way. The altar itself may be the ground or floor on which you perform the ritual. Or you may use a double cube (2' × 2' × 4' high), a coffee table, desk top, or a flat bottomed basket. Use whatever is available to you at home. A chest of drawers would make an ideal altar space as ritual supplies could be stored in a drawer. However, make sure they are separate from everyday clothing and other non-ritual items. Whatever you decide to use should always be cleaned before starting the ritual. If you decide to use the floor (and this is perfectly permissible), it is highly recommended that you use an altar cloth (such as a clean white handkerchief) or a mat specifically reserved for that purpose. This will help to buffer your ritual objects from the more mundane vibrations of the floor or ground. You may wish to keep a notebook beside your altar to record your subjective experiences and the objective aspects of your ritual for future reference.

Altar arrangements may be simple or elaborate, according to personal preference. A typical altar arrangement might be one candle, incense, and a bowl of water on a clean, white handkerchief (*i.e.*, the altar cloth). The simplest altar arrangement would be a single candle; this can be as effective as any other altar display. See figure 6 on page 32 for a typical altar layout.

As you continue in ritual work, you might wish to add other psychic aids to your altar, such as:

An Altarpiece. This is usually a symbolic picture or statue representing that to which or to whom you pray—Christ, a pagan god, Egyptian ankh, Tibetan mandala, crystal ball.

Elemental Tools. Some people prefer to use a sword for air, wand for fire, cup for water, and pentacle for earth. Others prefer using a fan, incense, water and salt. Elemental tools should be placed on the east, south, west, and north segments of the altar, respectively.

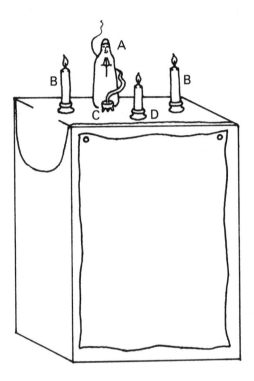

Figure 6. The Altar. This altar design shows a) an altarpiece, b) two divinity candles, c) an incense holder, and d) the standard desire candle. Behind the curtain on the front of the altar are shelves holding other ritual supplies (such as extra candles, incense, oils, herbs, notebook). A more permanent altar can be left set up against a wall (preferably facing east or north) and the circle can be invoked around yourself and the altar when performing a ritual. Or the altar can be moved each time to the center of a room where a larger circle can be invoked and visualized.

Extra Candles (see Candles and Incense, on page 35). Flowers, herbs, feathers, a bell, a rattle, a drum, meditation/new age music, or any other objects that you feel would help to channel the higher energies can be added to your altar at your discretion.

Everything you choose to place within your circle of light should be attractively arranged, contribute to the element of oneness, and be a purposeful ingredient in your ritual work.

Spirit Altar

A magically effective altar is set up by practitioners of Santeria (a Latin American mystery religion) called a "spirit altar." The adherents of the religion feel that one should pray to one's deceased ancestors before any other spiritual work is done. This is to insure that the deceased ancestors (now in spirit) make the way clear for other spiritual energies to come to you. You can simply pray that the ancestors are blessed in the light of God and then ask them for their blessings in your life (for health, happiness, financial security, love, spiritual understanding, protection). This might seem to be a morbid practice, but can eventually lead to a healthier attitude towards life and death, finally perceiving death as a continuum of life in another dimension. With the spirit altar and honoring your ancestors, you can receive spiritual inspiration and greater creative energy to perform other more specific rituals.

To create a spirit altar, simply set three or more glasses (or glass jars) of plain water in a triangular formation on a separate altar space. The center glass of water will represent God Almighty; traditionally, a crucifix is placed over or inside this glass to distinguish it from the others. The other glasses will represent the spirits of your translated ancestors. A white candle is placed in front of the center glass and it is lit each time the ancestors are to be worshipped. (See figure 7 on page 34.)

Figure 7. The Spirit Altar.

Ancestor worship can take place on a daily basis or it can be performed periodically (for example, once a week, preferably on Mondays). It is customary to kneel before the altar, light the candle, make the sign of the cross (if you are so inclined), recite the "Lord's Prayer" (or any other suitable invocation to the Highest in your philosophy), then bless the ancestors one by one. The ancestors are named individually, starting with the great grandparents; if the names are not known, "Great Grandmother" and "Great Grandfather" are acceptable.

Offerings can be made to the ancestors and other spirit helpers on the spirit altar. Fresh flowers (especially white flowers), candy, cooked rice, fresh fruit, coffee, alcoholic beverages, and cigar smoke are popular offerings. Place the offering on the altar after you have blessed the ancestors and leave it there so that the spirits can partake of the energy of the offering and help you spiritually. Don't overload the altar with offerings—something simple from time to time is fine. If fruit, flowers, or food (such as candy or cooked rice) is offered, remove the offering before any decomposition occurs (such as mold); in this way, you will feed only positive energy to spirit.

After you have blessed the ancestors and made an offering (optional), you can affirm blessings for those now living (including yourself), if you wish. Or, you can request special help with a particular problem, but don't overwork the spirit altar with problem-solving; it is perhaps best appreciated as a form of prayer meditation that psychodynamically prepares you for other ritual work.

The spirit altar ritual is a psychic battery charger and its effect is revitalizing. This ritual can be performed without the addition of other rituals and produce a very holistically healing influence in your life. It is not necessary to invoke the circle of light around your spirit altar before praying to the ancestors. The spirit altar can be kept against a wall, out of the way somewhere, undisturbed. The area around the altar should always be kept clean. This altar should not be used for everything else. If you are going to perform other rituals in addition to worshipping the ancestors, another altar space should be used. This other altar should be kept separate from the spirit altar.

Candles and Incense

Candlelight symbolizes spirit, the fire of the soul. In candlelight the mind is rendered receptive to spiritual energy. The psyche is thus aligned and a direct channel is created between the subtle, spiritual consciousness and the normal waking consciousness. Candlelight produces energy which can be used to produce effects through the spiritual plane onto the material plane of existence.

Candle color is very important. Each color has a specific effect on the psyche in terms of spiritual energy. And each spiritual energy responds to a specific color in a specific way. For example, the color gold is a symbol of wealth, success, illumination. Light a gold candle and those energies will be attracted to the illumined color. It is permissible to use an appropriately colored glass candle holder through which the candlelight would shine; in this way, the desired color of illumination would be produced. The Table of Correspondences lists the colors that correspond to the basic spiritual energies; however, here is a brief list of candle colors that can be used and the energies they will attract:

> *White*—Sincerity, Truth, Purity, God, Spirit,
>   Healing
> *Red*—Passion, Sex, Strength, Energy
> *Yellow*—Money, Friendship, Lovers, Upliftment,
>   Healing
> *Blue*—Peace, Compassion, Clairvoyance, Luck
> *Orange*—Mental Stimulation, Attraction, Adapt-
>   ability
> *Green*—Money, Fertility, Growth, Healing
> *Purple*—Magical or Financial Power, Clairvoyance
> *Pink*—Love, Harmony, Joy, Healing

If you do not have the appropriate colored candle for the spiritual energy you wish to contact, the color white may be substituted; however, the appropriate color is preferred. The desire candle (or spiritual energy candle) is placed in the middle of the altar or altar cloth. (See figure 2 on page 5)

Any type of candle may be used, as a votive or a taper. Avoid using candles made of animal oil. Anoint the candle with olive oil or an appropriate occult oil. (For anointing instructions, see figure 8, on page 37.) Occult supply shops usually carry specific types of anointing oils for specific purposes; otherwise, olive oil works very well. The anointing oil will hold whatever psychic charge is put into it. Once a candle has been anointed for a particular spiritual energy, it

Figure 8. Candle Anointing. To anoint the candle, hold it at its center, and, with the anointing oil, rub upwards to the top of the candle from its center. Then, still holding the candle at its center, rub downwards with the oil to the bottom of the candle. While you are performing this process, concentrate on the spiritual energy which the candle is to represent. Use an appropriate occult oil for the anointment, or use olive oil. If you do not have these oils, you may use vegetable oil.

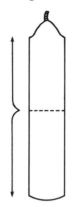

should only be burned to contact that energy. If you choose to perform a ritual for a number of days, on the last day of the ritual the desire candle should be burned all the way down. This rule also holds true if you are to perform the ritual for only one day. (See Ritual Timing on page 9). If the candle is made to burn several hours and you only make plans for a one hour ritual, you might use a smaller candle or simply cut a candle so that it will burn for the desired time.

In addition to the desire candle, other candles may be used in the circle. Four candles placed on the east, south, west, and north arcs of the circle represent the four elements: air, fire, water, and earth, respectively. The element candles can be all white. If you prefer, you can use colored candles as follows:

yellow for air—east
red for fire—south
blue for water—west;
white or green for earth—north.

The element candles are lit in a clockwise direction (as the circle is cast), starting in the east. Two tall, white candles placed outside the eastern periphery of the circle or on the east segment of the altar represent Divinity—the Father/Mother God Principle or the Alpha/Omega Principle. The two divinity candles are always the first to be lit (before the circle is cast) and the last to be extinguished (after the circle is dissolved). An appropriate invocation may be spoken when lighting the divinity candles, such as, "Heavenly Father and Holy Mother, let there be light," or, "Blessed is the light of spirit." The desire candle is the last to be lit and the first to be extinguished. (See figure 9.)

While candlelight engages the sense of sight in ritual, incense engages the sense of smell. Incense helps to induce the psychic atmosphere. As with candle color, there are specific aromatics that correspond with specific spiritual energies. Choose the type of incense that is best suited for the specific

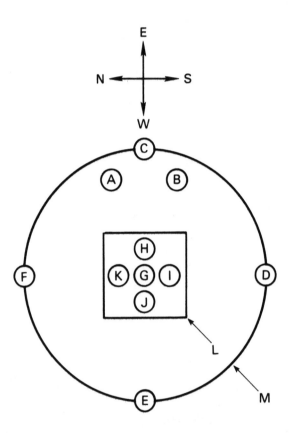

Figure 9. The circle, showing a complicated ritual format. A and B are Divinity candles; C, D, E and F are Element candles; G is a Desire candle; H is a fan (for air element); I is incense or candles (for fire element); J is your bowl or cup of water (for water element); K is a dish of salt or bread (for earth element); L is an altar or altar cloth; M represents the circle perimeter.

spiritual energy you wish to contact (see Table of Correspondences). If you don't have an incense that is best suited for the spiritual energy, then substitute one that is pleasant smelling. Use incense whenever possible. It should be burned in an appropriate censer for safety. The inexpensive brass or ceramic incense holders are fine. Light the incense in the beginning and let it burn throughout the ritual.

The Elements

In the ancient wisdom everything is composed of four basic elements: air, fire, water, and earth. Air represents the mind; fire represents the spirit; water represents the emotions; and earth represents the physical body. The four elements describe the four basic energies that comprise the cosmos as well as the individual. When these four elements are represented in the circle—either actually or symbolically—a greater balance of the energies is effected. The inner mind realizes these energies, and, when they are applied in ritual, a greater channel for spiritual energy is created. To represent the four elements in ritual is to speak the basic language of the cosmos. Spiritual energy is sometimes referred to as the "fifth" element or the astral light.

The four elements can be represented very simply: a hand fan may be used for the element of air; lighted incense for the element of fire; a bowl of water for the element of water; and a dish of bread or salt for the element of earth. These four items are placed on the altar or in the respective quadrants of the circle. In more advanced forms of ritual, there are specific applications for the elemental weapons; however, their simple presence in the circle helps to channel and balance those energies. Ceremonial magicians often invoke the four elements for extra power and protection while the circle is cast. Shamans refer to the four elements as the "four directions" or the "four winds." Hindus perceive the elements as the "four faces of Brahma." Further knowledge of the elements can be gained through the study of astrology and tarot.

Empowering Your Magic with Crystals

Clear quartz crystal is in vogue everywhere. Small crystals are worn as earrings, suspended on necklaces, or mounted on rings. The scientific world uses quartz in computers and the metaphysical world uses it in meditation and healing. Aboriginal peoples have used crystals for thousands of years in dreaming, conjurational magic, healing, telepathy, and trance work. A form of crystal, perhaps clear quartz, was largely responsible for the advanced technology of Atlantis, and wholly responsible for the destruction of the continent. Quartz crystals are inexpensive and readily available in nature as well as in mineral shops, new age bookstores, and occult supply outlets.

Crystals are physical representations of pure light and mental clarity. When used like a prism, they will produce the entire rainbow spectrum of light. Essentially, they are used as thought-energy transceivers and electro-magnetic devices that duplicate, magnify, and generate any type of thought or energy. (See figure 10.) Virtually, you can induce a crystal to generate whatever results you want. Simply breathe on the crystal as you mentally will your intention into it. Or, as you hold the crystal to your mouth (so that you are breathing on it), tell it specifically what you would like it to do.

Although clear quartz crystals can produce all the primary universal energies, they are highly individualistic and each seems to *specialize* in one kind of energy. If you decide to wear a crystal, it is wise to wear only one at a time. If two or more crystals are worn on the body, their energies could converge

Figure 10. Clear quartz crystal, showing the direction of energy flow.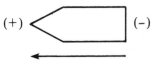

disharmoniously and create havoc in your personal energy field as well as in the world around you. Since crystals are very powerful, it is also a good idea to begin working with only one. Eventually, as you become accustomed to crystal energy, you can add more crystals to your retinue.

If you don't have a crystal, the best way to get one is for another person to give one to you, or for you to spontaneously find one in nature. This will tell you that the universe has decided you are truly ready to use this form of energy—and the crystal will be more cooperative than one you buy for yourself. Spiritual energy is not so easily bought or sold. However, don't let this stop you—you can buy a crystal, now, for experimentation purposes, if you don't have one. When you get a crystal, do the following:

1. Thank the crystal for coming to you (even if you bought it). Tell it (mentally or verbally) that you would like to work together in a cooperative manner.

2. Place the crystal in a glass of salt water for 24 hours to remove any past vibrations and thought forms.

3. Take the crystal to a natural water source where there is a rock that is half-in-and-half-out of the water. Tap the base end of the crystal against the rock. This process will *activate* the crystal and it will be ready for magical use.

4. Learn to intuit the kind of energy the crystal generates as an individual—such as cool, warm, masculine, feminine, dreamy, telepathic, fiery, airy, watery, earthy, or one of the planetary energies. When you have chosen an energy that seems to fit, use the crystal in modes that are congruous with its intrinsic energy. It will work better for you by using it in this way.

5. Carry the crystal with you in a pocket or a purse, or place it with some of your personal belongings from three to thirty days. Or, you may sleep with it under your pillow. (If you do, you may have some incredible dreams.) Keeping the crystal close to you will orient it to your personal vibrations.

There are many ways to use crystals magically. Here are a few workable suggestions, and you may have the delight of discovering many others:

Charging A Candle: You may use from one to four crystals for this. First, program the crystal by holding it in one or both hands. Then, as you visualize the spiritual energy color in and around the crystal, verbalize (or mentally will) your intention directly into the crystal. You may have to repeat the intention until you intuit that the crystal is saturated with the intention. For example: In a healing ritual using a green candle, visualize green light in and around the crystal and say, "Channel healing energy." When you have sufficiently programmed the crystal, place it pointing towards the candle (within a distance of one inch) in a quiet spot for three to seven days. (See figure 11.) After this time, the candle will be fully charged and ready to use in a magic ritual. If the directions are properly followed, the ritual will be powerful. To deprogram a crystal, place it in a glass of plain water overnight, or place it on a shelf somewhere for a few days. This will dissipate the energy and thought you have put into it.

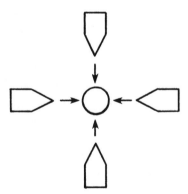

Figure 11. Using crystals to charge a candle (or other ritual tool).

Empowering A Ritual: Program the crystal(s) you will use with the appropriate spiritual energy color and ritual intention (as in *Charging a Candle*). Place the crystal(s) pointing away from the desire candle with the base of the crystal(s) within one inch of the candle base (see figure 12). Leave the crystal(s) in place as you perform a ritual. Crystals can be rather slow acting when they are programmed to generate a specific intention. It can take from three to seven days for a crystal to begin generating its full effects. In this case, you may want to repeat the ritual for a number of days.

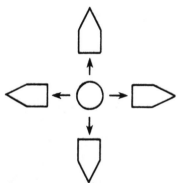

Figure 12. Using crystals to draw energy down into the candle (center) and outwards into the environment. Arrows show direction of energy flow.

Creating A Powerful Energy Vortex: Place four appropriately programmed crystals in a symmetrical formation, pointing in a counter-clockwise direction around the desire candle (see figure 13). This configuration will generate the spiritual energy from the center outwards in a spiral.

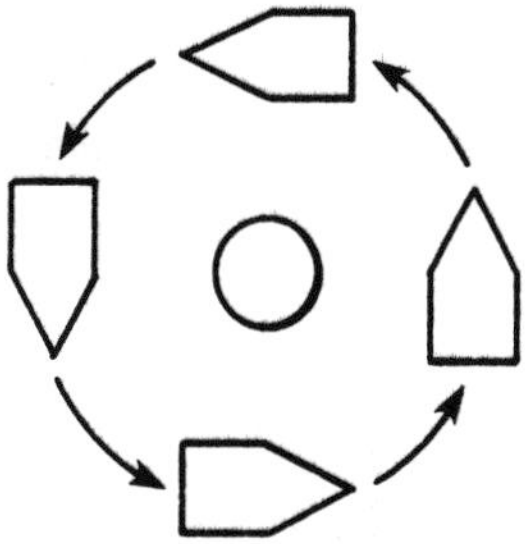

Figure 13. Creating a powerful outward spiraling energy vortex around a desire candle.

Review of Materia Magica

1. One object is most important in ritual—a candle representing the spiritual energy to be contacted.

2. The candle should be properly anointed and placed in the center of the circle on an altar or altar cloth, if possible.

3. Other items may be used which can help induce a more effective psychic atmosphere, as:

> *Incense:* Specific aromatics help to attract correspondent energies.

> *Extra Candles:* Element candles illumine the idea of the four elements; divinity candles illumine the idea of the divine. The subconscious mind, thereby rendered receptive to those ideas, helps to channel their energies in the circle.

> *Elemental Weapons:* There are four basic energies that comprise everything in this universe. When those energies are symbolized in the circle, a greater balance of energy is effected. The circle thereby becomes a more fertile ground on which spiritual energy can become manifest. The elements can be represented by: a hand fan for air; incense for fire; a bowl of water for water; and a dish of bread/salt for earth.

> *Crystals:* To create a powerful energy vortex and empower your magic.

4. Everything in the circle should be attractively arranged, purposeful, and contribute in some way to the concept of oneness.

4

Complete Ritual Outline

Now that you have studied the ritual techniques and concepts described in this book, you have the knowledge to design and execute a ritual that is tailored to fit your own specific and individual needs. It is time to put all this information together into an outline which you can follow for creating and performing your own rituals:

1. First, decide which spiritual energy and divine name will best fulfill your needs (refer to the Table of Correspondences on page 49).

2. Equip your ritual working area with the materials (candles, symbols, incense) that correspond with the spiritual energy and divine name you wish to contact (refer to Materia Magica on page 44 and the Table of Correspondences on page 49).

3. Take a salt water bath and/or smudge yourself prior to beginning the ritual (refer to Psychic Cleanliness on page 2).

4. Reverently enter the ritual working area and clearly state the specific intention of the ritual (refer to Ritual Format on page 6).

5. Light the two divinity candles—if they are to be used in your ritual (refer to Candles and Incense on page 35).

6. Cast the circle of light around your ritual working area (refer to The Circle of Light on page 3).

7. Sit, stand, or kneel facing east before your altar.

8. Silently contemplate the spiritual energy you wish to contact.

9. Light the desire candle (refer to Candles and Incense on page 35).

10. Make an invocation to the spiritual energy which the desire candle represents (refer to Ritual Format on page 6).

11. Imagine the spiritual energy entering your circle of light until you perceive that you have made contact (refer to Ritual Format on page 6).

12. Divinate (with cowry shells, coins, a pendulum, or playing cards) to determine which spiritual energy (if any) has entered your circle (refer to Divination—"Who is there?"—on page 13).

13. After you determine which spiritual energy is in the circle, divinate to ascertain why that particular energy has come to you (refer to Divination—"Why did you come?"—on page 14).

14. If the spiritual energy is in your circle to fulfill your original request, divinate to determine what you must do for the spiritual energy to grant your wish (refer to Divination—"What is needed from me to make this happen?"—on page 15).

15. If an offering is requested, make the offering immediately (if it is within your capacity to do so), then divinate to determine whether or not the offering is acceptable (refer to Divination—"Was the offering acceptable?"—on page 16).

16. If you get a "no" response from the divination question ("Was the offering acceptable?"), continue with the divination procedure by asking, "What more can I give you?"

17. When you get a "yes" response to the question, "Was the offering acceptable?", end the ritual: give thanks to the spiritual energy for entering your circle of light and granting your request.

18. Extinguish the desire candle.

19. Dissolve the circle of light (refer to Ritual Format on page 6).

20. Extinguish the two divinity candles—if they have been used.

21. Allow time for results to manifest. Place yourself in logical situations that will better allow your magic to work for you.

22. Repeat the ritual at another time if you deem it necessary (refer to Ritual Timing on page 9).

Overall Review

● Ritual work is an integrative process that attunes the psyche to natural forces.

● The natural forces, or spiritual energies, are brought forth in ritual through the use of symbols.

● The circle is a symbol of oneness, the universe. It is a bridge between two worlds, the spiritual and the material. The circle is the foundation of ritual work and the starting point of rituals.

● To contact a specific spiritual energy, an invocation is made and a candle is lit in the center of the circle. Candlelight symbolizes spirit.

● More specific communication can be made with the spiritual energy through divination. There are many forms of divination; any may be used and two or more forms of divination may be used together in ritual.

● To enhance the ritual process, other psychic aids may be used: altarpieces, extra candles, incense, drums, bells, rattles, recorded music, flowers, ceremonial robes, banners, colors. All can help, but none are absolutely necessary. Use whatever feels right, is purposeful, and contributes to the element of oneness.

● The Table of Correspondences is a general outline of spiritual energies with their correspondent genders, colors, days, numbers, planets, and divine names. To channel a specific energy, refer to the table.

5

Table of Correspondences

To use the table, first decide which spiritual energy describes your needs (refer to Spiritual Energies on page 55). Then, in the lists of correspondences beginning on page 62, locate the planet which governs the spiritual energy you will select. Listed under the planet will be the correspondent color, day, incense, number, polarity, tarot card, divine names, and symbols which you will need for the ritual you will perform. For example: a friend complains to you of depression and you wish to help alleviate the problem in some way. In the spiritual energies list, under "Psychological Development," you will find "joy." The governing planet for joy is Venus, as shown. On page 63, under "Venus," are the following correspondences:

Color: Green (Harmony), Pink (Love)
Day: Friday
Incense: Amber, Rose
Number: 6, 7
Polarity: Feminine
Tarot Card: The Empress (III)
Divine Names: Venus, Aphrodite, Hathor, Oshoun, Archangel Haniel, Divine Love.
Symbols: River, Rose, Honey, Dove, Magic Girdle, Flaming Torch, Seashell, Flaming Heart, Swan, Dolphin, Mirror, Copper, Emerald, Ruby, ♀.

Therefore, to help your friend out of the state of depression by inducing joy, you would perform a Venusian ritual. For the ritual, you would light a pink or green candle and amber or rose incense. The Empress (III) tarot card could be placed on your altar with one or more of the symbols listed (such as a piece of copper). One or more of the divine names listed would be invoked and the ritual would ideally begin on a Friday during the waxing moon (to *align* the energy of joy). The ritual could be repeated six or seven days in a row, or until your friend begins to truly experience joy.

Trust your own true feelings and intuitions to know the best representation of that spiritual energy you wish to channel. If this Table of Correspondences is not right for you, then choose other symbols, names, and correspondences for the energies you would like. If a tree symbolizes harmony for you, and you want more harmony in your life, then put a tree in your circle—an imaginary tree or a real one—and call upon the tree or the higher powers to bring you harmony. If you feel that starlight is the presence of god, put a symbol or picture of a star in your circle. Or, go outside on a clear night, then cast the circle of light around yourself, and pray to the stars directly. Since the dawn of time, people have been making pilgrimages to specific *power spots* throughout the world. It is wise to understand that a power spot is not just a representative of a specific energy or spiritual being, it actually *is* that energy or being. In Nigeria, the Yoruba people will go to the ocean and pray *directly to* the ocean as Yemaya, one of their goddesses, and leave little gifts of supplication there. To them, the ocean *is* Yemaya. The results from the rituals of the Yoruba people are often astounding. It spiritually behooves us all to become acquainted with the powers of nature as direct expressions of the spiritual energies we wish to contact and channel. There are limitless possibilities. Trust your intuition to be creative, with the admonition of common sense.

If the divine names do not appeal to you, then use another appropriate divine name or abstract concept that you like. You could use "absolute wisdom" in place of spiritual awareness,

"Lord Jesus" for protection, "love" for emotional healing, for example. In place of any of the divine names, you may also choose the name of the highest in your spiritual philosophy (such as God, Light, Love, Absolute Being, Oneness, Higher Self, Subconscious Mind).

If the application of the divine names seems too complex or unsuited to your philosophy, it is possible to create other subdivisions of the one light. The trinity or triune consciousness is one concept that could be used here. In this case, there are three main divisions or categories: the Divine Being (transcendent) principle; the mother/female (yin) principle; the father/male (yang) principle. All cool colors represent the yin principle; all warm colors represent the yang principle; and the color white (the balanced combination of all spectral colors) represents the transcendent principle. All matters pertaining to the spirit and mind would be dealt with under the yang principle; all matters pertaining to the emotions and physical body would be dealt with under the yin principle; and all matters pertaining to the divine light or higher mind (as blessings, healing, divine guidance/inspiration/union) would be dealt with under the transcendent principle. To petition the yin (female) principle, one could invoke "mother earth" or "holy mother." To petition the yang (male) principle, one could invoke "father sky" or "heavenly father." To petition the transcendent principle, one could invoke "ancient of ancients" or "transcendent light." Any pleasant-smelling incense may be used and the waxing and waning moon periods should be observed for ritual timing, if possible.

There are a number of symbols listed for each planetary correspondence. Although it is not necessary to use any of the symbols listed to get the results you want, you may find that, by placing one or more appropriate symbols on your altar or in your circle of light, you will become more visually or more tangibly involved with the spiritual energy which you will invoke. However, if you create a parade for the senses by cluttering your ritual space with symbols, you are apt to become subconsciously confused by the array. To remain one-pointed in your effort, a few symbols will be sufficient. For example, in a ritual to spread loving vibrations to a world in need, a rose, a seashell, and a photograph of some dolphins on an altar sounds lovely. To create a meditational touch in the arrangement, one might add The Empress (III) tarot card. If you cannot obtain the actual symbol listed, a tasteful drawing or a photograph is fine (real dolphins are apt to be unwieldy participants in any ritual!).

The tarot cards listed are pictographic representations of the specific spiritual energies. To magically use a tarot card, first place the card in a central location on your altar, cast the circle of light around your working space as you have been instructed, then relax and contemplate the card for about five minutes. Simply notice the colors, shapes, and other symbols on the card; easily let the various characteristics of the card sink into your awareness. And let your awareness sink into the card. There is no need for you to consciously understand the meaning of the card and its symbols, for it will be the subconscious mind that will do all of the work of understanding and responding to the spiritual energy that the card represents. When you feel ready to begin, place the card in an unobtrusive, yet visible position on your altar, and follow the standard ritual format for the spiritual energy with which you will work.

The table can also be used for color visualization. Select the color that corresponds to the spiritual energy you want. Simply visualize that color as a sphere of light around the person, place, or thing you wish to effect (even if it is yourself). An affirmation better defines and increases the power of the visualization. For example, perhaps it would be inconvenient for you to perform a ritual for your friend who is depressed. You would simply visualize the color pink or rose (for "joy") around your friend using a suitable affirmation such as, "In the name of Venus, I affirm joy in the life of [friend's name] now." Of course you would want to get your friend's permission before helping with a problem that did not belong to you. In this way, you would not be so apt to get tied up in your friend's karma. If the friend did not like the idea of "ritual," you could say a prayer to help out (everybody likes to be prayed for unless they are very superstitious or staunch atheists).

Whenever doing anything magical for anybody else, always consider what it is you are really doing. If it seems that you are really trying to control another person rather than giving a magical helping hand (for instance, with a little boost of good energy), *then stop what you are doing.* To try to harness the will of another is interfering with that person's birthright which is *free will.* To do so is to interfere with divine will and the mess you make could cause you a great deal of personal confusion and hardship at a later date. Always take into consideration the magical premise, "As you give, so shall you receive."

Use the visualization technique at intervals until the problem is solved; trust your intuition to know when and how long to visualize; verbally affirm the spiritual energy each time you use its color. You can also use this technique around a pet. Visualization can be applied anytime, anywhere; it is not necessary to follow a particular time schedule. All that is required is your ability to concentrate and visualize clear, unmuddied colors.

The colors indicated in this table are spectral colors, which, combined equally, produce pure, white light. All the colors are individual aspects or qualities of the first emanation (white light/brilliance) and should be considered so at all times. During a color visualization, incense may be burned, but it is not necessary. You might wish to experiment with the effects of color (as they express or imply specific spiritual energies) in a painting.

This table is a general outline of esoteric concepts and definitions. It is not impervious to change, deletion, or revision. With deft research and wisdom you can make additions to this table or create your own. Some areas of study that would help in your research are: astrology, tarot, cabala, color symbolism, religions (ancient and modern), and

Shamanism. The Suggested Reading List on page 65 provides sources for further study.

The divine names of the gods and goddesses that are listed here were derived from several pantheons. They are:

Roman: Saturn, Jupiter, Mars, Apollo, Venus, Mercury, Diana.

Greek: Kronos, Zeus, Ares, Helios, Aphrodite, Hermes, Artemis.

Hebrew (Archangels): Metatron, Tzaphkiel, Tzadkiel, Khamael, Raphael, Haniel, Michael, Gabriel.

Egyptian: Anubis, Maat, Horus, Ra, Hathor, Thoth, Isis.

Yoruba: Olofi, Babalou-Ai-Ye, Yemaya, Obatala, Oshoun, Chango, Ellegua, Ogoun.

The reader should be aware that color and number correspondences for the Yoruba gods and goddesses may differ from the other pantheons listed in the Table of Correspondences. If you work with the Yoruba pantheon, use the attributes listed in Table 1. Although the attributes of the Yoruba deities are similar to the attributes of the other gods listed in the Table of Correspondences, it is wise to become initiated into the Yoruba magical system before invoking the virtues of its gods. The Yoruba deities are direct expressions of primal (though highly sophisticated) forces in nature. To invoke them in an uninitiated mode might serve only to deface their inherent majesty and grace. I am including the Yoruba pantheon to help readers who are aware of other magical systems. However, if you are meant to become initiated into the Yoruba mysteries, and include its gods in your magical format, it is believed that the *orisha* (Yoruba gods) will help you find a true priest or priestess of the religion in order to be instructed in their system.

When you invoke a spiritual energy described in this book, it is reasonable to use one, several, or all of the divine names listed for that particular spiritual energy. Other pantheons may be substituted as you see fit; however,

Table 1. Yoruba Color and Number Correspondences

Divine Name	Color	Number
Obatala	White	8
Babalou-Ai-Ye	Black/Brown/Green	9
Yemaya	Blue & White/Purple	7
Oshoun	Yellow	5
Chango	Red & White	6
Ellegua	Red & Black	3
Ogoun	Green & Black	3

especially in the beginning phases of your work, it is better to become oriented to one, specific pantheon of gods and goddesses than to psychically bounce around from one culture to another. Take the time to learn the various aspects (properties, myths, and symbols) of the deities of one particular culture that is especially attractive to you. In this way, you will enrich your understanding of the magical psychodynamics involved when you perform a ritual. Eventually, as you gain mastery of the material presented here, you will discover whether or not eclecticism is for you. When you are ready to broaden your magical base of working, you will naturally begin to include other cultures in your repertoire.

Spiritual Energies

From the following lists, select the spiritual energy that you will conjure in your ritual. Then refer to the Planetary Correspondences on page 62 for the remaining ritual symbology. If there is more than one planet listed with the spiritual energy you select, you must intuitively decide which planetary correspondence will best meet your needs. (In this case, you may refer to the Table of Correspondences for further guidance.)

Magical Power and Abilities

Blessings: Trans-Saturnian, Jupiter
Ceremonial Magic: Mercury
Conquering Evil: Trans-Saturnian, Sun
Divine Protection: Trans-Saturnian, Jupiter
Magical Power: Jupiter
Magical Skills: Mercury
Messenger to the Gods: Mercury
Nature Magic: Venus
Priesthood: Jupiter
Secrets: Saturn, Moon

Psychic Development

Clairvoyance: Jupiter
Disincarnate Spirits: Trans-Saturnian, Moon
Divination: Mercury
Dreams: Moon
Higher Self: Sun
Lower Self: Moon
New Age Abilities: Jupiter
Protection: Trans-Saturnian, Saturn, Jupiter, Sun
Psychic Development: Moon
Secrets: Saturn, Moon
Soul Power: Sun
Spirit Guide: Trans-Saturnian, Sun, Moon
Spiritualized Intellect: Sun
Trance Channeling: Trans-Saturnian, Jupiter, Sun, Moon
Truth: Trans-Saturnian, Jupiter
White Light: Trans-Saturnian

Spiritual Development

Absolute Infinity: Trans-Saturnian
Almighty God: Trans-Saturnian
Buddha/Christ Consciousness: Trans-Saturnian
Divine Guidance/Power/Union: Trans-Saturnian
God Manifest: Sun

Goddess Manifest: Moon
Higher Self: Trans-Saturnian, Sun
Holy Ghost: Saturn
Illumination: Trans-Saturnian, Sun
Initiation: Sun, Moon
Inspiration: Trans-Saturnian, Jupiter
Meditation: Trans-Saturnian, Jupiter, Sun, Moon
Perfection: Trans-Saturnian
Purity: Trans-Saturnian
Reflection: Saturn
Saintliness: Trans-Saturnian, Jupiter
Spiritual Aspiration: Moon
Spiritual Devotion: Jupiter
Spiritualized Intellect: Sun
White Light: Trans-Saturnian

Health and Healing

Adult Female: Moon
Adult Male: Sun
Balance: Venus
Children: Mercury
Elderly People: Saturn
Emotional Healing: Venus, Moon
Illness: Saturn
Maternity: Moon
Medicine: Sun, Mercury
Mental Healing: Sun, Mercury
Nature Rhythms: Venus
New Life Energy: Venus
Physical Healing: Trans-Saturnian, Sun, Venus, Mercury, Moon
Physical Stimulation: Mars, Mercury
Purification: Trans-Saturnian, Mercury
Spiritual Healing: Trans-Saturnian, Jupiter, Sun
Vitality: Sun, Mercury
Yang: Sun
Yin: Moon

Psychological Development

Anger: Mars
Assertiveness: Mars
Balance: Venus
Change: Mercury
Cheerfulness: Sun, Mercury
Conquering Evil: Trans-Saturnian, Sun
Counsel: Jupiter
Dreams: Moon
Emotions: Moon
Feelings: Moon
Femininity: Moon
Freedom of Thought: Mercury
Growth: Venus
Happiness: Sun, Venus, Mercury
Harmony: Venus
Illumination: Sun
Inspiration: Jupiter
Joy: Venus
Light-Heartedness: Mercury
Love: Venus
Masculinity: Sun
Moods: Moon
Popularity: Sun, Mercury, Moon
Resistance: Mars
Sexuality: Mercury
Sociability: Mercury
Sorrow: Saturn
Soul Power: Sun
Spiritualized Intellect: Sun
Subconscious Mind: Moon
Superconscious Mind: Sun
Sympathy: Moon
Well-Being: Venus

Transpersonal Idealism

Agape: Trans-Saturnian, Sun
Balance: Venus

Brotherhood: Venus
Compassion: Moon
Detached Idealism: Saturn
High Aspiration: Moon
Honors: Jupiter
Mercy: Trans-Saturnian, Jupiter
Peace: Trans-Saturnian, Jupiter, Venus, Moon
Sisterhood: Venus
Understanding: Moon
Universal Love: Venus

Financial Power and Wealth

Abundance: Venus
Commerce: Mercury
Expansion: Jupiter, Mercury
Financial Power: Jupiter
Gold: Sun
Growth: Venus
Inspiration: Jupiter
Leadership: Sun, Jupiter
Luck: Jupiter, Venus
Luxury: Venus
Money: Jupiter, Sun, Venus, Mercury
Opportunity: Mercury
Promotion: Sun
Royalty: Jupiter
Silver: Moon
Success: Sun
Victory: Venus
Wealth: Jupiter
Wishes: Moon

Creative Expression

Art: Sun, Venus
Creative Expression: Jupiter
Dance: Venus
Drama: Sun

Education: Mercury
Freedom of Thought: Mercury
Inspiration: Jupiter
Intellectual Stimulation: Mercury
Invention: Jupiter
Music: Sun, Mercury
New Age Ideas: Jupiter
New Ideas: Mercury
Publishing: Jupiter
Science: Jupiter
Skills: Mercury
Truth: Jupiter
Writing: Jupiter, Mercury

Materialistic Powers

Authority: Sun
Balance: Venus
Battle: Mars
Buildings: Jupiter
Career: Sun, Mercury
Change: Mercury
Crystallization: Saturn
Doors: Mercury
Home Life: Moon
Houses: Moon
Justice: Mars
Karma: Saturn
Laws of Manifestation: Saturn
Material Harmony: Venus
Materiality: Saturn
Occupation: Mercury
Physical Peace: Venus
Physical Property: Saturn
Physical Power: Mars, Sun
Protection: Trans-Saturnian, Saturn, Jupiter, Sun
Resistance: Mars

Restriction of Activity: Saturn
Roads: Mercury
Silence: Saturn
Survival Instinct: Mars
Time: Saturn
Travel: Mercury

Powers of Nature

Day: Sun
Fertility: Moon
Hunting: Moon
Lightening: Jupiter, Sun
Mountains: Jupiter
Nature: Venus
Night: Saturn, Moon
Ocean: Moon
Pathways: Mercury
Rain: Venus
Rivers: Venus
Snow: Jupiter
Storms: Jupiter

Love and Romance

Desire: Venus, Moon
Emotions: Moon
Feminine Beauty/Love: Venus
Happiness: Sun, Venus, Mercury
Harmony: Venus
Love: Venus
Lovers: Sun, Venus
Loyalty: Jupiter
Matrimony: Moon
Masculine Beauty/Love: Sun
Romance: Venus

Planetary Correspondences

Trans-Saturnian Planets

Color: White (Purity)
Day: All
Incense: Frankincense, Myrrh, Sage, Rosemary
Number: All
Polarity: None
Tarot Card: The Fool (0)
Divine Names: Holy of Holies, Ancient of Ancients, Great Spirit, God, Allah, Christ, Mohammed, Krishna, Olofi, Obatala, Heavenly Father/Holy Mother, Higher Self, Archangel Metatron, Divine Light
Symbols: Sky, Star, Eagle, Lightning, Mountains, Lamb, Fish, Rainbow, Lotus, Light, Flame, Butterfly, Ankh, Equal-Armed Cross, Sideways Figure Eight, Mandala, Wheel, Circle, Yin-Yang, Star of David, Stone, Clear Quartz Crystal, Diamond, Eye, ⊕.

Saturn

Color: Indigo (Absorption)
Day: Saturday
Incense: Myrrh, Musk
Number: 3, 4
Polarity: Feminine
Tarot Card: The Universe (XXI)
Divine Names: Saturn, Kronos, Anubis, Babalou-Ai-Ye, Archangel Tzaphkiel, Divine Silence
Symbols: Scythe, Crutch, Ouroborous, Clock, Lead, Onyx, ♄.

Jupiter

Color: Blue (Peace), Purple (Power)
Day: Thursday
Incense: Cedarwood, Frankincense, Juniper, Nutmeg
Number: 4, 5
Polarity: Masculine

Tarot Card: Wheel of Fortune (X)
Divine Names: Jupiter, Zeus, El, Maat, Obatala, Archangel
  Tzadkiel, Divine Power
Symbols: Sky, Eagle, Mountain, Thunderbolt, Tin, Lapis
  Lazuli, Sapphire, ♃.

Mars

Color: Red (Stimulation)
Day: Tuesday
Incense: Dragon's Blood, Tobacco
Number: 3, 9
Polarity: Masculine
Tarot Card: The Tower (XVI)
Divine Names: Mars, Ares, Horus, Ogoun, Archangel
  Khamael, Divine Will
Symbols: Helmet and Shield, Spear, Sword, Cauldron, Wolf,
  Ram, Iron, Bloodstone, ♂.

Sun

Color: Yellow (Illumination), Orange (Freedom), Gold (Up-
  liftment)
Day: Sunday
Incense: Frankincense, Cinnamon, Vanilla
Number: 1, 6
Polarity: Masculine
Tarot Card: The Sun (XIX)
Divine Names: Sol, Helios, Apollo, Ra, Chango, Archangel
  Raphael, Divine Wisdom
Symbols: Crucifixion, Halo, Shepherds' Crook, Globe, Bow,
  Scarab, Double-Headed Axe, Arrow, Quiver, Snake, Swan,
  Lion, Fire, Lyre, Gold, ☉.

Venus

Color: Green (Harmony), Pink (Love)
Day: Friday
Incense: Amber, Rose

Number: 6, 7
Polarity: Feminine
Tarot Card: The Empress (III)
Divine Names: Venus, Aphrodite, Hathor, Oshoun, Archangel Haniel, Divine Love
Symbols: River, Rose, Honey, Dove, Magic Girdle, Flaming Torch, Seashell, Flaming Heart, Swan, Dolphin, Mirror, Copper, Emerald, Ruby, ♀.

Mercury

Color: Orange (Freedom), Yellow (Illumination)
Day: Wednesday
Incense: Sandalwood, Lavender, Fennel, Tobacco
Number: 5, 8
Polarity: Hermaphroditic
Tarot Card: The Magician (II)
Divine Names: Mercury, Hermes, Thoth, Ellegua, Archangel Michael, Divine Knowledge
Symbols: Caduceus, Magic Wand, Winged Sandals, Winged Hat, Coin Purse, Lyre, Roads, Cowry Shells, Quicksilver, Opal, Agate, ☿.

Moon

Color: White (Completion), Pale Blue (Compassion), Violet (Inspiration)
Day: Monday
Incense: Jasmine
Number: 2, 7, 9
Polarity: Feminine
Tarot Card: The High Priestess (II)
Divine Names: Luna, Diana, Artemis, Isis, Yemaya, Archangel Gabriel, Divine Patience.
Symbols: Ocean, Bow and Quiver, Spear, Veil, Shield, Crescent, Stag, Dog, Silver, Moonstone, Pearl, ☽.

Suggested Reading List

The following list of books may help you expand your present understanding of ritual:

Ritual Book of Magic, Clifford Bias, Samuel Weiser, Inc., York Beach, ME, 1981. A practical compendium of ritual magic forms.

The Magician: His Training and Work, William Butler, Wilshire Book Co., Hollywood, CA, 1969. Clear and rich insights of the inner workings in magic and ritual. Energy tides.

The Hero with a Thousand Faces, Joseph Campbell, Princeton University Press, Princeton, NJ, 1973. Myths and universal themes spanning many cultures.

A Guide to the Gods, Richard Carlyon, William Morrow and Co., Inc., New York, 1982. The gods of Africa, America, Asia, Europe, the Middle East, and Oceania are listed individually and described.

The Ancient Art of Color Therapy, Linda Clark, Pocket Books, New York, 1978. Color symbolism and its application in day-to-day living.

The Magical Philosophy, Volumes I-V, Melita Denning and Osborne Phillips, Llewellyn Publications, St. Paul, MN, 1975. A thorough treatment of ritual as performed in the Western Mystery Tradition. Information on energy tides.

Psychic Self Defense and Well-Being, Melita Denning and Osborne Phillips, Llewellyn Publications, St. Paul, MN, 1980. Information on the psychic world that every occultist should know.

Mystical Qabalah, Dion Fortune, Samuel Weiser, Inc., York Beach, ME, 1983. A classic work. The Qabalah, or Tree of Life, is a system of classifying and correlating the primal energies of creation.

Creative Visualization, Shakti Gawain, Whatever Publishing, Mill Valley, CA, 1982. Visualization is an important part of ritual. The basics of visualization as well as special techniques are explained in clear, simple language.

The Santeria Experience, Migene Gonzalez-Wippler, Prentice-Hall, Inc., Englewood Cliffs, NJ, 1982. Ms. Gonzalez-Wippler colorfully recounts her lifelong experiences with the Yoruba gods and Santeria (the Latin American version of the Yoruba mystery religion).

Therapeutic Metaphor, David Gordon, Meta Publications, Cupertino, CA, 1978. "The purpose of this book is to provide you with skills which will enable you to formulate and effectively use therapeutic metaphors." The world of metaphysics often portrays ritual magic as a form of sympathetic magic; whereas, the world of psychology describes ritual, mythology, and religion as psychodynamic metaphor. (Ritual works, regardless of what you call it.) Pay special attention to the sections on synesthesia: there is a wealth of information that can be rewardingly incorporated into your magical format.

A Complete Guide to the Tarot, Eden Gray, Bantam Books, New York, 1982. An exceptionally clear and insightful presentation of tarot. Also, it explains how tarot, astrology, numerology, and cabala are correlated.

Trance-formations, John Grinder and Richard Bandler, Real People Press, Moab, UT, 1981. Neuro-linguistic programming and the structure of hypnosis. Although ritual magic is not discussed, this book will give the reader insight into how ritual is effective from a psychological viewpoint.

The Way of the Shaman, Michael Harner, Bantam Books, New York, 1982. A guide to ritualistic power and healing techniques as practiced by South American Indian shamans.

The Brotherhood of Angels and Men, Geoffrey Hodson, The Theosophical Publishing House, Wheaton, IL, 1982. A most inspiring guidebook for contacting celestial beings.

The Seven Keys to Color Healing, Roland Hunt, Harper and Row, New York, 1982. Color symbolism and its application.

Man and His Symbols, Carl Jung, Dell Publishing Co., Inc., New York, 1964. A psychological treatise of universal symbols.

The Magical Temple, Michael Kearton, The Aquarian Press, Wellingborough, England, 1980. A practical guide for the creation of a personal sanctuary.

Imagineering For Health: Serge King, The Theosophical Publishing House, Wheaton, IL, 1981. Excellent compendium of mental exercises derived from the Huna Science. Greater mental or psychic ability can produce more effective results in ritual.

Kahuna Healing, Serge King, The Theosophical Publishing House, Wheaton, IL, 1983. Delves into the mysteries of Huna and brings it more to light. Serge King is a kahuna.

Self Awareness Through Huna, Erika Nau, The Donning Company, Publishers, Virginia Beach/Norfolk, VA, 1981. A comprehensive guidebook for understanding and applying the principles of Huna as a practical science. Instructions on how to clear away blocked energy.

The Art and Practice of Getting Material Things Through Creative Visualization, Ophiel, Samuel Weiser, Inc.,York Beach, ME, 1980. The mechanics of creative visualization are elucidated by a practiced magician.

Ceremonial Magic, Israel Regardie, The Aquarian Press, Wellingborough, England, 1980. A guide to the mechanics of specific ceremonial magic rituals. Core rituals, as practiced by members of the Order of the Golden Dawn (a Western Mystery School), are given.

The Tree of Life, Israel Regardie, Samuel Weiser, Inc., York Beach, ME, 1980. A classic work. A persuasive treatise on the "high objective" of magic by a world authority.

Voluntary Controls, Jack Schwarz, E.P. Dutton, New York, 1978. Creative meditation, reverie, clearing the psychic channels (chakras) for greater receptivity to the Higher Creative Intelligence.

The Spiral Dance, Starhawk, Harper and Row, New York, 1978. The much misunderstood practices of witchcraft are delineated in a positive light, with emphasis on healing and energy alignment with the cosmos.

The Twelve Rays, James Sturzaker, Aquarian Press, Wellingborough, England, 1981. Color Symbolism.

Incense, Leo Vinci, Aquarian Press, Wellingborough, England, 1980. All about incense and its use in ritual. Also contains recipes for preparing incense.